THE WITCH OF BLACKBIRD POND

by
Elizabeth George Speare

Teacher Guide

Written by:
Anne Troy

Note

The Dell Yearling paperback edition of the book was used to prepare this teacher guide. The page references may differ in the hardcover or other paperback editions.

ISBN 1-56137-246-3

To order, contact your local school supply store, or—

Novel Units, Inc.
P.O. Box 791610
San Antonio, TX 78279

Table of Contents

Skills and Strategies

Thinking
Brainstorming, classifying
and categorizing, evaluating,
analyzing details,
comparing and contrasting,
synthesizing ideas

Vocabulary
Words in context, prefixes/
suffixes, root words

Comprehension
Predicting, sequencing,
cause/effect, inference,
comparing information from
more than one source

Writing
Narrative, journal, report
writing

Listening/Speaking
Participation in discussion,
debate

Literary Elements
Character, setting, plot
development, point of view,
figurative language, foreshadowing, conflict

Summary of The Witch of Blackbird Pond:
Orphaned Kit Tyler arrives from Barbados unannounced at the home of her aunt and uncle in the Connecticut Colony. Awaiting her in the new home were suspicions and loneliness. Her uncle did not like anything she said, did or believed. There was no one who understood her or tried to help her except the strange lady outside the village boundaries. Thus Kit suffered guilt by association with the Witch of Blackbird Pond.

Instructions Prior to Reading:
You may wish to choose one or more of the following prereading discussion questions/ activities. Each is designed to help students draw from their store of background knowledge about the events and themes they will meet in the story they are about to read.

Prereading Activities:
1. **Previewing:** Have students examine the title and cover illustration. What can you tell about the time period of the story by the girl's clothes? What does the girl's expression tell you about her feelings? Why do you think she is in the woods? What do you predict the story will be about?

2. **Background on Witchcraft in the American Colonies:** (To be provided to students, or researched by them.) Witchcraft is the use of supposed magic powers. A witch is a person who has received these powers from evil spirits and uses them to harm people or their property.

   During the seventeenth and eighteenth centuries, the fear of witchcraft was widespread in Europe. Thousands of people were tried and executed as witches. Many kinds of tests were used to determine if the person was a witch. American colonists, influenced by European beliefs and practices, persecuted many women. In Salem, Massachusetts, the most famous witch hunt occurred. The Massachusetts colonists executed 20 people and imprisoned 150 others. The courts allowed gossip, rumors, and even the testimony of children against their parents to be used as evidence in court.

3. **Concept Map:** Write "**WITCHCRAFT**" at the center of a large piece of paper, to be kept for later comparison with events in the book (or as a bulletin board display to be expanded as the story is read). Have students generate any ideas that come to mind when they hear the word. Jot the ideas around the word, helping students organize them into categories such as synonyms, antonyms, types and examples. Draw "wagon spokes" around the central concept ("**WITCHCRAFT**") to connect it with the supporting ideas (categories). Encourage students to add to the chart during and after their reading of the novel.

Definition: Magic practiced in league with the devil.

4. Do a concept map for "**COURAGE**."

5. Given certain word clues, what might happen in this novel: Witchcraft, ship, Puritan, sailors, orphan?

6. *The Witch of Blackbird Pond* is an example of historical fiction. In historical fiction, the main characters are usually creations of the writer's imagination (although real people may appear or be mentioned in the story). The setting is real--usually a time and place which had historical importance. Help students fill in the chart, below, comparing and contrasting historical fiction with history.

	Historical Fiction	History (Factual)
Setting:	Our world	Our world
Characters:	May or may not be people who really lived	People who really lived
Action:	Could have happened but not entirely true story	True story
Problem:	Could have belonged to someone living at the time of the story	Real problem
Examples:	*My Brother Sam Is Dead* (Collier)	*Hiroshima* (Hersey)
	Johnny Tremain (Forbes)	*Dawn* (Wiesel)

Using Predictions in the Novel Unit Approach

We all make predictions as we read—little guesses about what will happen next, how the conflict will be resolved, which details given by the author will be important to the plot, which details will help to fill in our sense of a character. Students should be encouraged to predict, to make sensible guesses. As students work on predictions, these discussion questions can be used to guide them: What are some of the ways to predict? What is the process of a sophisticated reader's thinking and predicting? What clues does an author give us to help us in making our predictions? Why are some predictions more likely than others?

A predicting chart is for students to record their predictions. As each subsequent chapter is discussed, you can review and correct previous predictions. This procedure serves to focus on predictions and to review the stories.

Use the facts and ideas the author gives.

Use your own knowledge.

Use new information that may cause you to change your mind.

Predictions:

_____

_____

_____

_____

Prediction Chart

What characters have we met so far?	What is the conflict in the story?	What are your predictions?	Why did you make those predictions?

Chapter 1 - Pages 1-14

Vocabulary:

pinnaces 2	retching 2	disembark 4
tedious 4	prow 5	hawser 5
repulsed 6	anguish 7	impulsively 8
vicious 8	daft 9	retorted 9
defiantly 10	warrant 11	quirked 12
diverted 12	curdle 13	taunted 13
nonchalance 14		

Vocabulary Activities:

1. Select ten words. Write only every other letter and a synonym or definition. Exchange student papers. Example: a_o_a: smell (aroma).

2. One student picks a word from the vocabulary list. Another student has ten (or 5) questions to discover the word and give the definition.

Discussion Questions:

1. Locate Connecticut and Barbados on a map. Approximately how many miles did Kit travel?

2. The setting in this novel is important. Why do you think the author contrasts Connecticut's dreary gray harbor with Barbados?

3. The author introduces and describes many characters in the first chapter. Make a list of them and their physical and personality characteristics.

4. Why did Kit jump into the water? *(Page 8, to get a child's doll)* What do we learn about Kit through this incident? *(Pages 8-10, Kit is impulsive.)* How else might Kit have retrieved the doll without diving for it?

5. Begin an attribute web for Kit. What have we learned about her? (See pages 9-11.) *(brave; can swim; sympathized with a child; is from Barbados, West Indies; orphan; lived with grandfather; rich because she had maids)*

6. A story map is an outline that helps you to understand and remember the story better. What do you know about the story after reading only the first chapter? Fill in the story map that follows on page 12. Add to it as you read each chapter.

Using Character Webs—in the Novel Unit Approach

Attribute Webs are simply a visual representation of a character from the novel. They provide a systematic way for the students to organize and recap the information they have about a particular character. Attribute webs may be used after reading the novel to recapitulate information about a particular character or completed gradually as information unfolds, done individually, or finished as a group project.

One type of character attribute web uses these divisions:

● How a character acts and feels. (How does the character feel in this picture? How would you feel if this happened to you? How do you think the character feels?)

● How a character looks. (Close your eyes and picture the character. Describe him to me.)

● Where a character lives. (Where and when does the character live?)

● How others feel about the character. (How does another specific character feel about our character?)

In group discussion about the student attribute webs and specific characters, the teacher can ask for backup proof from the novel. You can also include inferential thinking.

Attribute webs need not be confined to characters. They may also be used to organize information about a concept, object or place.

Attribute Web

The attribute web below is designed to help you gather clues the author provides about what a character is like. Fill in the blanks with words and phrases which tell how the character acts and looks, as well as what the character says and what others say about him or her.

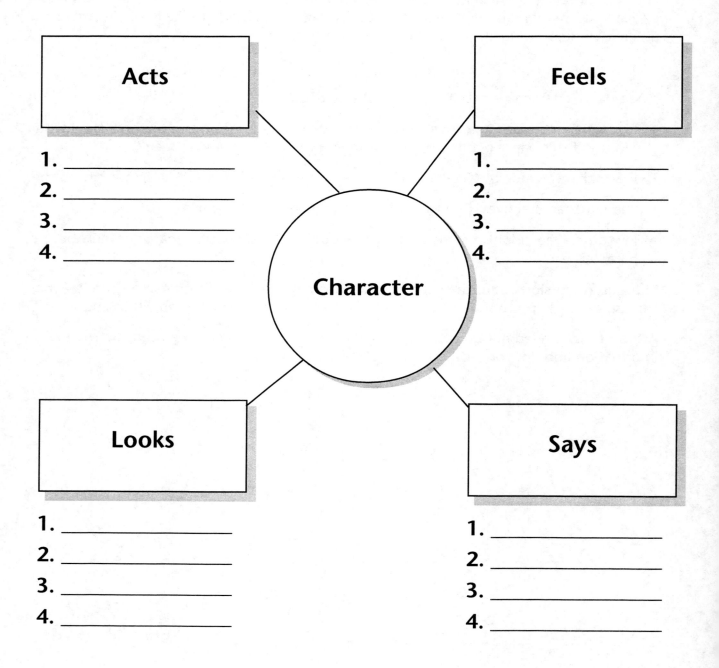

Acts

1. _____
2. _____
3. _____
4. _____

Feels

1. _____
2. _____
3. _____
4. _____

Character

Looks

1. _____
2. _____
3. _____
4. _____

Says

1. _____
2. _____
3. _____
4. _____

Attribute Web

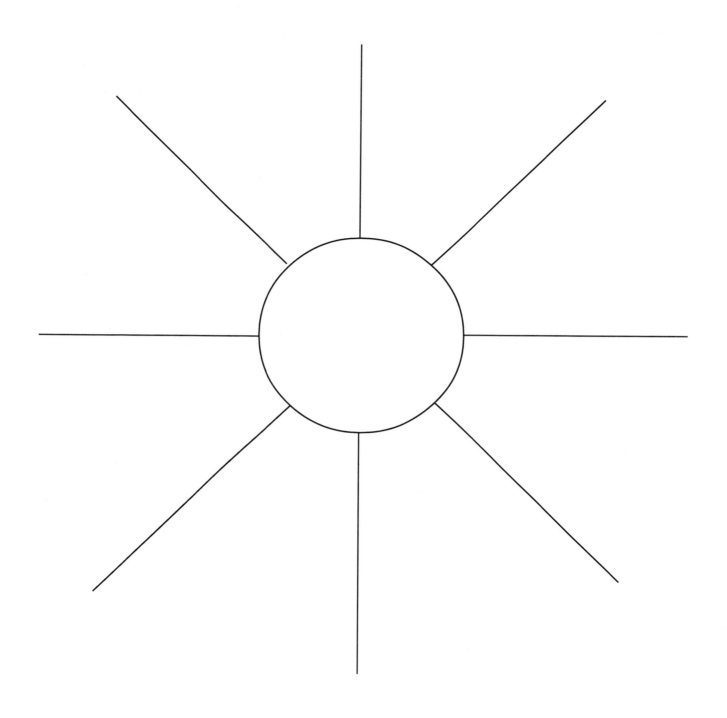

Story Map

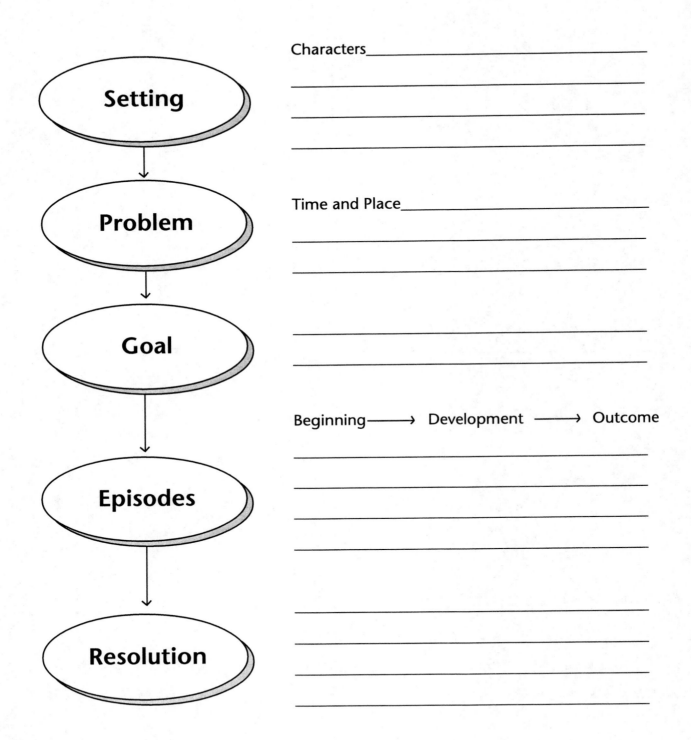

Characters_____
_____
_____
_____

Time and Place_____
_____
_____

_____
_____

Beginning ⟶ Development ⟶ Outcome
_____
_____
_____
_____

_____
_____
_____

7. Why did Goodwife Cruff think Kit was a witch? Why do you think beliefs about witches developed? *(Pages 13-14)*

8. Brainstorm the meaning of Puritan. *(People were not happy with rule by the King of England; wanted to "purify" the Church of England; did not welcome people with different ideas; education was important because it was necessary to read the Bible; believed plays and poetry were sinful; believed fancy clothes and pretty colors were wrong.)*

9. After the class brainstorms the word Puritan as a group, students will complete research sheet on Puritans on page 14.

10. What products was the ship bringing to the Colonies? Why were the products on the ship important to the Colonies? *(Page 3, Sugar and molasses; the Colonies had no other source of sugar or molasses; these food stuffs improved their food supplies.)*

11. What did Nat and John Holbrook warn Kit about and why? *(Pages 12-13, People in Connecticut were different from Barbados. They believed that only witches could swim.)*

Prediction:
What do you think this sentence could mean, "There was something strange about this country of America, something that they all seemed to share and understand and she did not"?

Supplementary Activities:
1. **Writing:** Begin a journal in which you react to each section of the story you read. Reactions might include: Questions you have about the story; memories the story evokes; people or other stories of whom characters remind you; judgments about whether you agree or disagree with what characters have done; your thoughts about topics which come up such as loneliness, courage, heroism, etc. Try some times including vocabulary words from the story in your journal.

2. **Writing:** Assume the role of Kit. After reading each section, jot down an entry about what has happened and how you feel about it in your "diary."

3. **Literary Analysis--Point of View:** Writers can tell their stories from many points of view. Sometimes a central character in the story tells the story. Sometimes the storyteller is a minor character. Sometimes the storyteller is a narrator who can see inside of the characters. And sometimes the writer shifts the point of view from one person to another. Who tells most of the story of *The Witch of Blackbird Pond?* *(an all-seeing narrator)*

Puritan Research Sheet

Puritans

Who were they?   (People who disapproved of the many practices of the Church of

England.)

_____

_____

_____

_____

*Why did they come
to New England?*
into   (Hoped to establish a community where they could put Christian ideals

practice; hard for Puritan farmers to make a living in England because of

high taxes; King of England , Charles I, persecuted Puritans; condemned

and sentenced Puritans without benefit of jury trials.)

_____

_____

*Where was the first
Puritan Colony?*   (Boston)

What was it called?   (Massachusetts Bay Colony)

Chapter 2 - Pages 14-28

Vocabulary:

tantalize 15	wraith 16	stingy 16
furtively 16	shrew 16	punctilious 17
quizzical 17	begrudge 17	scandalized 19
intangible 20	imperceptibly 21	incautiously 22
constraint 22	impulsively 24	dominion 24
incredulous 25	cherished 25	reproof 25
cavernous 26	befell 28	

Discussion Questions:

1. Begin an attribute web for John Holbrook. *(studying to be a minister; too poor to go to Harvard; likes to read)*

2. What did "walking up the river" mean? *(Page 21, Sailors walked along the shore and pulled a rope attached to the boat to move it forward when there was insufficient wind.)*

3. Why did the Eatons bring horses on their boats rather than slaves? *(Page 23, Did not believe in bringing half-dead slaves from Africa. Considered slavery wrong.)*

4. How did Kit view slavery? *(Page 23, Probably had not thought much about what slavery meant. "How else could you work a plantation?")*

5. Why was John Holbrook shocked that Kit read plays? *(Page 24-25, Most girls never learned to read. Puritans believed plays were sinful.)*

Prediction:

What kind of reception will Kit get from her aunt and uncle?

Supplementary Activities:

1. **Literary Analysis:** Sometimes an author uses a **simile** to help the reader form an image. A simile is a comparison between two things. A simile usually uses <u>like</u> or <u>as</u>.

   A **metaphor** suggests a comparison by saying one thing is another without using like or as.

Personification is used when a writer gives human characteristics to an animal or object.

Keep a running list of similes, metaphors and personification as you read the book. Illustrate or draw pictures of the two objects being compared.

2. **Comprehension Strategy--Inference:** Sometimes you are given clues about an event in the story, and you must put the clues together--like pieces of a jigsaw puzzle--to figure out what has happened or what will happen.

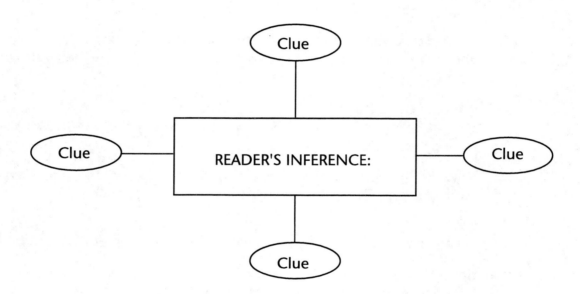

Chapter 3 - Pages 29-38

Vocabulary:

burnished 32	angular 32	grotesquely 33
nondescript 33	regal 35	instinctive 36
pondering 36	impulse 36	conceded 38

Vocabulary Activities:

1. Draw pictures to remember the definition.

2. Play charades to dramatize words.

3. Place the words for the day in categories, e.g.:

Descriptive	War Words	Feelings
pudgy		monotonous
vicious		irksome

Actions	Things	Person
devise	pinnaces	shrew
writhe	prow	hypocrite

Categories may be added as new words are introduced. The lists will be displayed during the entire novel.

4. Vocabulary "Bee": The teacher (or student-teacher) gives a definition and a student supplies the word. The game is played like a spelling bee. This may be played in cooperative groups with the student-teacher using an answer key.

5. Students may pick two words from the displayed lists and tell how they might be related.

6. Students will make predictions about how the author will use vocabulary to tell about the setting, characters, the problem or goal, the actions, resolution, or feeling of a character in a story. (Blanchowicz, 1986, *Enhancing Comprehension Through Vocabulary Development.*)

Discussion Questions:
1. The author develops characters using contrasts. How were Judith and Mercy physically different? Use a T Diagram to compare.

Judith	Mercy
• clear skin	• gray eyes
• blue eyes	• twisted, crooked body
• dark eyes and hair	• beautiful smile
• very pretty	

2. Why did Kit not write to her aunt before she came? *(Pages 36-37, She was afraid that they might tell her not to come and she would have to go someplace else.)*

3. Why did Kit's statement shock her uncle, "To pay my way on the ship I had to sell my own Negro girl"? *(Page 37, He did not believe in slavery and he realized that Kit had no money.)*

4. What if Kit had acted haughty and like the wealthy? How would her reception have been different?

Prediction:
What problems will Kit have with her new family? What clues do you find in this chapter? What inferences might the reader make?

Supplementary Activities:
1. **Research:** Royalist, Roundhead, or traitors who murdered King Charles.

2. **Research:** Compare and contrast the climate and landscape of Connecticut with that of Barbados.

3. **Art:** Have students create a bulletin board display depicting the characters they meet in the book, complete with the clothing or props which identify each. For example, students should research what Kit's aunt and uncle probably looked like and then draw them.

4. **Art:** Choose part of the story which is not illustrated, but which you feel should be. Use the medium of your choice (markers, crayons, paints, collage) to illustrate that scene.

5. **Language Study:** Make a list of all the terms that refer to clothing, weapons, events, etc. which mark the story as taking place during the Colonial period (and not today). Three examples: pewter mug, wooden plate, homespun.

Chapter 4 - Pages 38-50

Vocabulary:

fend 38	chagrined 41	tremulous 42
intimidated 43	frippery 43	perceptibly 44
indigo 46	deft 46	misshapen 46
pudgy 47	gingerly 48	devise 48
irksome 48	writhe 48	monotonous 49

Discussion Questions:

1. How are the sisters Judith and Mercy different in temperament and behavior? *(Judith doesn't think her mother should do so much for others. Mercy is charitable and believes in her mother's good works. Judith envies Kit's beautiful clothes. Judith is sulky and rebellious. Judith looks like her mother did years before.)*

2. Why did Matthew Wood react so negatively to his wife and daughter's enjoyment of Kit's clothes? *(Page 43, because he is a Puritan; interruptions in work)*

3. What were the reasons Kit came to the Woods? *(Page 47, because she had no other relatives or money and because an old man wanted to marry her)* What else might she have done?

Supplementary Activities:

1. **Research:** Have the students complete word webs to show the kinds of work done by colonial women and men.

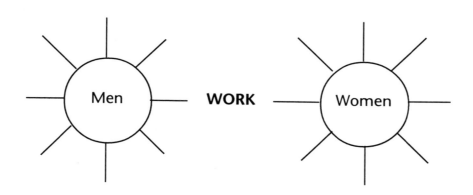

hunting; farming; salted meat; caring for animals; blacksmith made farm equipment; built houses

quilting; making soap/candles; cooking/cleaning; washing; making cheese/butter; preserving food

2. **Research:** Cloth production in the colonial period. Vocabulary: cording; indigo; weaving; skein.

Chapter 5 - Pages 50-59

Vocabulary:

affront 51	baffled 51	placating 51
auspiciously 52	aghast 52	turret 52
impact 53	undulated 54	convulsed 54
menacingly 54	venomous 55	staidness 55
demurely 56		

Discussion Questions:

1. What were some of the rules or customs at the Meeting House? *(Pages 52-53, Men sat on one side of building and women on the other; long sermons; everyone had to attend; women wore plain blue homespun clothes; two services on Sunday.)*

2. Why did Kit not like the worship service?

3. What does "set your cap for him" mean? *(Page 58, try to flirt with a young man in hopes of marrying him)*

4. How do the interests of Judith and Kit differ? *(Page 58, Judith is interested in marriage and Kit spends time thinking about avoiding marriage.)*

Prediction:
How will the two young men John Holbrook and William Ashby be important in the story?

Supplementary Activities:

1. **Art:** Draw a diagram of the village. Locate the Meeting House, pillory, whipping post, and stocks. As the story develops add: South Road, Great Meadow, Hannah Tupper's house, and Blackbird Pond.

2. **Research:** Stocks, pillory and whipping post. How were they constructed? How often were they used? How many settlements had them?

Chapter 6 - Pages 59-67

Vocabulary:

warrant 59	notorious 60	condescension 60
revolution 61	coddle 62	pompous 62
opinionated 62	canny 63	cadence 63
inexorably 63	appraisal 63	pivot 64
timorous 64	hypocrite 65	constrained 66
placid 66		

Discussion Questions:

1. Why and what did Reverend Bulkeley and Matthew Wood disagree about? *(Pages 60-62, loyalty to King James of England and the governor of Massachusetts)*

2. What is Matthew Wood referring to when he says, "He is a hypocrite and a whited sepulcher"? *(Page 65, Biblical reference; says one thing, does another. Sepulcher-- beautiful on the outside and on the inside--a rotting body.)*

3. Explain what is meant by William Ashby's permission to pay respects to Kit. *(Page 65, to begin courting or considering her for marriage)*

4. Why do you think Judith decided to set her cap for John Holbrook?

5. What did Kit mean when she said that, "Mercy was the pivot about whom the whole household moved"? *(Page 64, "She coaxed her father out of his bitter moods, upheld her timorous and anxious mother, gently restrained her rebellious sister and had reached to draw an uncertain alien in the circle.")*

Supplementary Activity:
Research: Steps in courting in the Colonies. Develop a chart contrasting courting in 1700 and dating today.

Chapter 7 - Pages 67-74

Vocabulary:

infectious 69	implacable 73	calculated 74
veritable 74		

Vocabulary Activities:

1. The students will use the vocabulary words from the chapter to make crossword puzzles on graph paper. They will write a question for each word and develop an answer sheet.

2. List vocabulary words on large sheets of paper. Leave space for students to a) illustrate the meaning next to each word; b) list a memory device to remember the word.

Discussion Questions:

1. How did Matthew Wood differ in his beliefs from William? *(Pages 70-71, William is afraid of angering the King about unclaimed land.)*

2. What was the only thing that William had to offer Kit through marriage? *(Page 74, The only way out of hard work of cleaning, scrubbing, weeding, and preparing wool.)*

Supplementary Activities:
1. Complete the Decision-making Grid on page 23 for Kit. Should Kit marry William as a way to get out of her uncle and aunt's household?

2. Develop a Characterization Chart with class participation. Characterization Chart: Characters are developed by what they say, think, and do, and by how others in the novel react to them.

   a) What is a heroine? List five words that describe Kit. Explain why she is a heroine. Are there other heroes or heroines in the novel? Name them.

   b) For each of the characters in this chart, describe when they experience the feelings listed. List other feelings.

Feeling	Kit	Matthew	Mercy	Judith	Hannah	William
frustration						
anger						
relief						
joy						
fear						
humiliation						
pride						
loneliness						

Decision-making Grid

The decision-making grid below is supposed to make it easier to find the best solution to a problem. Give examples of other questions you should ask yourself when you are trying to "weigh" different solutions. Then fill in the grid for the following problem: My best friend has been telling lies about me. See if classmates agree with the solution you decide is best.

Problem	Criterion #1	Criterion #2	Criterion #3
State the problem.	Will the solution hurt someone?	Will it make me feel better?	
Solution #1			
Solution #2			
Solution #3			
Solution #4			

3. As the novel is completed, develop a setting chart. The setting is the when and where of the novel, and includes the social environment. Often the setting contributes to the mood, or feeling, of the story.

   a) Locate examples which describe Wethersfield--the houses, the weather, the history, and the attitudes.

   b) Examine the function of the setting by completing the following chart.

Setting	Description	Dramatic Value
Wood's House	solid, respectable, glass windows	dreary
Town of Wethersfield	dirt road, rough cabins, not a single stone building or shop	depressing
Church		
Meadows		
Woods		
Village Square		
Hannah's House		

Chapter 8 - Pages 75-82

Vocabulary:

menial 75   encroaching 78   finicky 78
dubiously 80   rankled 81

Vocabulary Activity:
Words in Context: Ask students to "guess" at the meaning from context, telling <u>why</u> for each guess. Make a list of "why answers" to teach context clues.

Discussion Questions:
1. Foreshadowing is to present an indication or suggestion of something beforehand. What do you think could be foreshadowed in "never...would the Meadows break the promise they held for her..."? *(Page 77)*

2. What do you learn about the title of the book in this chapter? Why do you think this will be important?

3. What does the Meadow represent to Kit? *(Pages 76-77)* Describe a place that is like the Meadow to you.

4. What was a dame school? *(Pages 79-80, A primary school where small children learned their letters and to write their names.)* Why was this job appealing to Kit?

5. What does Mercy imply about the second baby boy's death? *(Page 81, He might not have died if Matthew Wood had not taken him to Church when it was so cold and he was so little.)*

Prediction:
How will the clues--the witch's house and the dame school--affect Kit's life?

Supplementary Activity:
Writing: Using this story as a model, try your hand at writing your own piece of historical fiction. If you like, choose your main character and time period from the suggestions below.

Main Character: A boy or girl your age, a teacher, a parent, a soldier, a doctor, a farmer, an animal

Time Period: The Dark Ages, any wartime, colonial America, the Industrial Revolution, the Depression

Chapter 9 - Pages 82-97

Vocabulary:

precarious 85	ingenious 85	enthralled 86
masque 86	obstreperous 87	vengeance 88
sanctioned 88	raiment 88	bedlam 88
floundered 89	incredulously 89	loiterers 90
ravenous 92	tangibly 93	incoherent 95
rapierlike 96	conjured 97	

Discussion Questions:

1. Why were Mr. Eleazer Kimberley and Reverend Woodbridge disturbed about Kit's dame school? *(Page 89, She was using play acting to teach Bible stories. The children were having a good time at school.)*

2. What clues did the author give us about Hannah Tupper? *(Page 94, odd shaped scar on her forehead; piece of coral)* What could these clues mean?

3. Why did Kit come to the Meadow? *(because she was upset)* What did Kit admit to Hannah? *(Pages 95-96, She was homesick for Barbados and her former happy life.)*

4. Why do you think Hannah showed Kit the beautiful flower that grew from a bulb from Africa? *(Page 96)* How was that flower a symbol for Kit? A symbol is something that represents something else by association.

Prediction:

Why do you think Kit went to Eleazer Kimberley's house?

Supplementary Activities:

1. **Literary Analysis--Background Information on Character for the Teacher:** The author may present his characters **directly** or **indirectly**. In direct presentation he tells us straight out what a character is like or has someone else in the story tell us what he is like.

   In indirect presentation, the author shows us the character in action; we infer what he is like from what he thinks, says or does.

   To be convincing, characterization, must also observe three other principles--first, characters must be **consistent** in their behavior. They must not behave one way on one occasion and a different way on another unless there is a sufficient reason for change.

Second, characters must be clearly **motivated** in whatever they do, especially when there is any change in behavior.

Third, characters must be **plausible** or **lifelike**.

Change in character:

- •must be within the possibilities of character who makes it.
- •must be sufficiently motivated by circumstances in which character finds himself.
- •must be allowed sufficient time for change to believably take place.

2. **Research:** Dress of Puritan children--little boys wore long dresses just like girls.

Chapter 10 - Pages 98-110

Vocabulary:

malicious 99	impassive 101	disclosure 101
invariably 102	baiting 102	diligently 102
unorthodox 102	skein 105	indignant 105
reproof 106	conjured 106	rapturously 107

Discussion Questions:

1. What other attributes can you add to Kit's web? *(brave, creative, ingenious)*

2. What did Rachel know about Quakers? *(Page 99, Stubborn people who didn't believe in the Sacraments. They were tormented and hanged in Boston.)* What generalization could we make about people who are prejudiced? *(They do not know very much about the topic or people they oppose.)*

3. Why do you think Kit went back to visit Hannah? What does the visit say about Kit's character?

4. Why did Hannah have to pay taxes on swamp land and fines for not going to a Meeting? *(Page 105)* What kind of work did Hannah do to pay the taxes and for whom did she do the work? What does this say about the Puritan community? *(Page 105, She was a branded Quaker and the Puritans who brought work to a "witch" were hypocrites.)*

5. How did both Nat and Kit find Hannah? *(Both of them were running away from trouble and crying in the Meadow.)*

Supplementary Activity:

Research: The triangle trade route--Molasses made in the West Indies was shipped to Colonial ports, where it was turned into rum. Rum and iron products were shipped to Africa where they were traded for slaves. The slaves were carried to the West Indies and to the Southern Colonies.

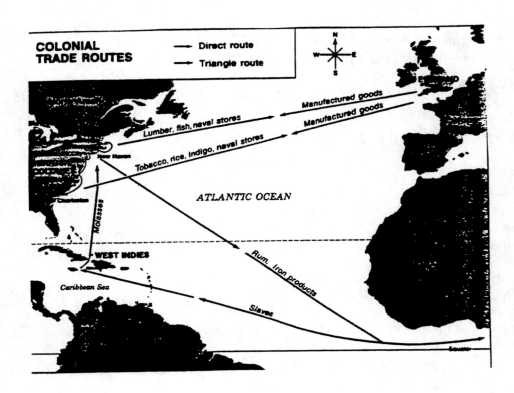

1. What goods were shipped from New England to England? *(lumber, fish, and naval stores)*

2. What goods were shipped from Charleston to England? *(tobacco, rice, indigo, and naval stores)*

3. What islands in the Caribbean Sea were the destination for ships sailing from Africa? *(West Indies-Barbados)*

Chapter 11 - Pages 111-122

Vocabulary:

exasperation 111
filigree 114
flair 119
discern 120

dreary 112
resolutely 116
adroit 119
resin 121

docilely 112
qualms 118
retrieve 120
incredibly 122

Vocabulary Activity:
Match each of the definitions with a word from the vocabulary list above.

irritation; annoyance; vexation *(exasperation)*

gloomy; cheerless; comfortless *(dreary)*

steadfastly; determinedly; unflinchingly *(resolutely)*

uneasiness; misgiving; scruples *(qualms)*

recover; regain; rescue *(retrieve)*

Discussion Questions:
1. How does Mercy accept being crippled? *(Page 112, She thinks about all the things she can do.)* What descriptive words can we add to Mercy's web?

2. Why do you think the author brought Prudence into the story?

3. When did we first meet Prudence? *(when she dropped her doll overboard into the water)*

4. How did Prudence get Kit into trouble in the first incident?

Prediction:
What trouble could Prudence cause this time?

Supplementary Activity:
Moral Level Chart: Lawrence Kohlberg is a psychologist who developed a model of moral development to explain what motivates an individual to act as he or she does. Kohlberg believes that his model can be applied to individuals of any culture.

There are six levels of moral development in his model. All people do not reach the highest levels. Decide which level best describes each character in Chapter 11. By the end of the novel, have these characters changed? How does this change show on a moral development chart?

Level I   Act to avoid pain or punishment
Level II   Act to get a reward
Level III   Act to gain approval
Level IV   Act because of belief in the law
Level V   Act for the welfare of others
Level VI   Act because of self-formulated set of principles

Character	Level	Reason
Kit		
Matthew		
Hannah		

Chapter 12 - Pages 122-133

Vocabulary:

quizzical 125   scythe 126   tangible 126
treason 129

Discussion Questions:

1. Why did Nat compare Kit to the bright colored bird he wanted to bring to his grandmother in Saybrook? *(Page 127, Kit, like the bird, was not meant to live among the cold Puritans. The other birds would scold and peck at it and not leave it alone.)*

2. What did Nat mean by two sides to loyalty? *(Page 129, "If the King respects our rights and keeps his word to us, then he will retain our loyalty. But if he revokes the laws he has made and tacks and comes about till the ship is on her beam ends, then finally we will be forced to cut the hawser.")*

3. What does Nat mean by the last part of his statement? *(Page 129, If the King makes too many changes in the law, the people will break away from England in a revolution.)*

4. What belief did Nat and Matthew Wood hold in common? *(Page 130, A man's first loyalty is to the soil he stands on.)* Do you believe they are guilty of treason? Why or why not?

Prediction:
Will Uncle Matthew's command to never visit Hannah change Kit's behavior? If you were Kit, what would you do?

Supplementary Activity:
Research: Do some research on colonial recipes and prepare a dish for the last day activities for this book.

Chapter 13- Pages 133-146

Vocabulary:

blithely 133	propitious 135	infatuated 135
rapturously 139	jubilant 140	exasperatingly 141
provocatively 141	impetuously 142	irresistible 142
brazen 142	forfeit 146	

Vocabulary Activity:
Each student will choose two vocabulary words. The student will write two sentences omitting the vocabulary words. Sentences will be read aloud and classmates will guess the correct word to complete the sentences.

Discussion Questions:
1. There is another foreshadowing of trouble for Kit because of Hannah Tupper. *(Page 137)* Who is the most important character in this novel? Defend your position.

The Most Important Character

Kit	Hannah Tupper

2. A protagonist is a leading character of a story. An antagonist is a character who works against the leading character. In this novel who is the protagonist and the antagonist?

3. What does the reader learn about John Holbrook in this chapter? *(Pages 136-137, Listens to the opinions of Dr. Bulkeley; is afraid Kit will be hurt by association with Hannah; plans to marry Mercy but is too weak; befuddled to resist Judith's entrapment.)*

4. What does Judith mean by "He'll never be able to find his tongue if I don't help him out"? *(Page 135)*

5. What did Hannah mean when she said "She's just hungry for more to read"? *(Page 136)*

Prediction:
What will happen to the young people in this story? Who will marry whom? What will happen to Hannah?

Supplementary Activities:
1. **Research Witchcraft:** What were the witches in the New England-Salem witch trials accused of? How were they punished?

2. **Writing:** List all class responses to prediction questions. Students will write their own conclusions to the novel.

Chapter 14 - Pages 146-153

Vocabulary:

buoyancy 147   barnacles 148

Discussion Questions:
1. In many instances Kit has not been impressed by her uncle or his behavior. What do you think she learned about his character by watching him in the garden? *(Page 147)*

2. What did Nat mean when he said "To think I worried about that little bird. I might have known it would gobble up a nice fat partridge in no time"? Who is the bird and who is the partridge? Why did Nat speak with "biting mockery"? *(Page 151, The little bird Nat refers to is Kit. The rich William Ashby is the partridge. Nat speaks withbiting mockery because he is jealous.)*

3. How had Governor Andros of Massachusetts saved Kit? *(Page 152, Discussion of the governor's moves to take the charter away distracted the group and forestalled additional questions from Judith.)*

Prediction:
What will the talk be about in the company room?

Chapter 15 - Pages 153-163

Vocabulary:

seething 154
dragoons 157
elated 163

chagrined 154
grenadiers 158
insubordination 163

brusquely 156
cavalier 159

Vocabulary Activity:
In cooperative groups or pairs, have students develop word maps for the vocabulary words using the following form. Use different color markers. Display.

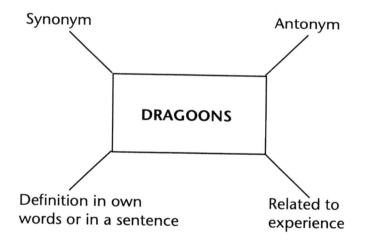

Discussion Questions:
1. Why did William begin thinking politically like Matthew Wood? *(Page 154, when he had to pay high taxes on his land)*

2. What do you think happened to the charter when the candles were blown out? Why was it important to the colonists to have the hidden charter? *(Pages 160-161, Men took the charter and they would keep it hidden until such a time they would begin again to resist the King.)*

3. What did Kit begin to admire in Matthew Wood? *(Page 162, "There was a sort of magnificence about him...she was proud of him.")*

Prediction:
What alternatives do the King and the colonists have?

Supplementary Activities:
1. **Debate** the colonists' point of view versus the King's. Organize the arguments for both sides.

2. **Literary Analysis--Character Relationships:** Think about the relationships each of the characters in the book has with the others. Complete the "sociogram" on the next page. Label each arrow with a word or phrase that describes the relationship (tells how the two people feel about one another or how they act toward each other).

3. **Literary Analysis--Point of View:** To get a better understanding of how the point of view affects a story, tell each of the following sections of the story from the given point of view.

    • Pretend you are Governor Andros. Describe what he saw and what he thought happened.

    • Pretend you are William. You are courting Kit but you spend much of your time talking to Judith.

    • You are Mrs. Wood. You don't think all this trouble with the King and Governor will change the colonists' lives much. It will spoil the Thanksgiving holiday.

Sociogram

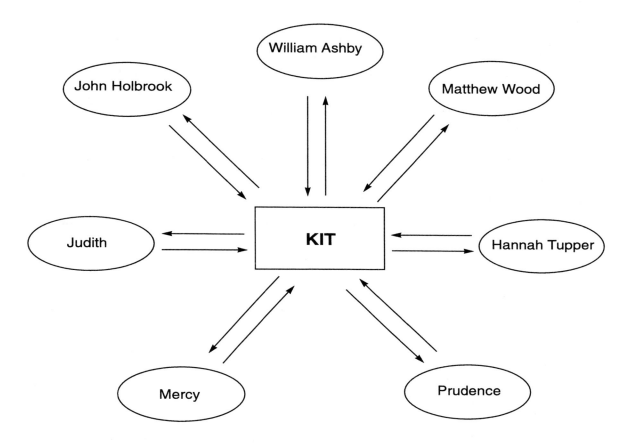

Chapter 16 - Pages 163-177

Vocabulary:

papist 164	roistering 165	blasphemy 165
culprits 166	repentance 166	pillory 168
banished 169	devious 169	ruefully 171
woebegone 172	tryst 172	retribution 172
ingenuity 173	premonition 175	poignant 175

Discussion Questions:

1. In some stories there are turning points where all the parts of the plot begin to come together. There is a main plot and several sub-plots in *The Witch of Blackbird Pond*.
   a) What do you think the main plot is? *(Kit versus Puritan community.)*
   b) What are the sub-plots? *(Hannah and witchcraft; romance; Kit and William and Nat; Mercy and John and Judith; William and Kit and Judith; Prudence and Kit.)*

2. Sub-plots are sequences of events partly distinct from the main plot. Often the form of a sub-plot parallels that of another section of the plot, so as to point up its significance by contrast or similarity.

3. Point of View: How would Matthew have told the story of Kit? How would Judith have told the story of Kit? How would Nat have told the story of Kit? What would each of them have added that Kit could not?

4. There are various kinds of conflict. **Internal conflict** between two desires within a character and **external conflict** between characters or between character and his environment. Give an example of each type of conflict.

5. The author has given clues or foreshadowings of events. What do you think these events foreshadowed?

   • Jack-o-lanterns
   • Nat in the stocks
   • Meetings of Prudence, Hannah and Kit
   • Prudence learning to write

6. What did Hannah mean when she said, "remember, thee has never escaped at all if love is not there"? *(Page 170)*

7. Why did others say John enlisted in the militia? Why do you think he did? How did this affect Judith?

   (Page 176, " 'Tis a doctor they needed, and John has learned a good deal of medicine..."

   Page 176, "...it was his way of breaking with Dr. Bulkeley."

   Page 177, John wanted to go away to prove something to himself. All Judith's plans for marrying John and building a house would have to be postponed.)

Supplementary Activity:
Research: All Hallows Eve, All Saints Day, Jack-o-lanterns.

Chapter 17 - Pages 177-194

Vocabulary:

attribute 177	poultice 181	consternation 181
consorting 182	infidel 183	slanders 183
frantic 184	clamor 186	serenity 188
wraithlike 190	tantalizingly 190	docile 191
obstinate 191	writhing 192	

Discussion Questions:

1. Why do you think the mysterious fever brought out the villagers' prejudices and fears about Hannah? *(Pages 177-181)* Can you name a mob action in modern times that is like the mob action of the villagers? How were the crowd actions alike and different?

2. What descriptive words can we add to Kit's web after she rescues Hannah?

3. Do you think it was too contrived to have the Dolphin and Nat arrive just in time to save Hannah from the mob and Kit from the problem of bringing her into the Wood's home where Matthew would have the duty to turn Hannah over to the law? List your arguments for and against this turn in the story. *(Page 190)*

4. If you were Kit, would you have taken Nat's offer to go to the West Indies? Why or why not?

Prediction:
What will happen to Kit?

Chapter 18 - Pages 194-206

Vocabulary:

contempt 197	chagrined 200	banished 203
blanched 203	magistrate 203	vengeance 205
flouting 205	inveigled 205	

Vocabulary Activities:

1. Decide what other prefixes and suffixes may be added to vocabulary words and note how these change the word meanings.

2. Create a word search for others to decode.

3. Do a word sort:

   <u>Nouns</u>   <u>Action Words</u>   <u>Describing Words--Adjectives-Adverbs</u>

Discussion Questions:

1. Kit has begun to see another side of Matthew Wood. When Kit thanks him for trying to prevent the witch hunt and standing up for her, what can we say about Kit's character and about Matthew Wood? Are they believable? Do they act like real people? Why? How does Aunt Rachel act?

2. Why do you think William doesn't come forward to save Kit from being imprisoned in the shed?

Chapter 19 - Pages 207-224

Vocabulary:

dubious 207	precaution 208	instigation 209
sundry 209	alleged 210	mutely 215
restraints 215	pandemonium 215	pinnace 223
slander 224		

Discussion Questions:

1. What is Kit accused of? *(Page 210, Being a friend of Hannah's and learning witchcraft from Hannah; causing the illness and death in the village.)*

2. Make a web to describe Prudence Cruff. How is her name Prudence ironic? What is irony? *(A figure of speech in which the literal meaning is the opposite of that intended. Prudent means shrewd, cautious, sensible, discreet. Prudence was not all these things when she learned to read at Hannah's house.)*

3. What Prudence reads from the Bible has an effect on her father. Put the quotation on page 220 in your own words.

Chapter 20 - Pages 224-238

Vocabulary:

reverent 225	surreptitiously 231	etched 234
arduous 235	gaunt 238	tremulously 238

Discussion Questions:

1. Why did William say he had not come during Kit's time of imprisonment and trouble? *(Page 227, because of illness in the house)* What was his real reason? *(Page 229, "We're judged by the company we keep. And in our position people look to us for an example of what is right and proper." William did not want Kit to associate with Hannah and Prudence. He was uneasy with the thought that he would never know what Kit would do next.)*

2. Why do you think Kit decided to return to Barbados? *(Page 237, Cold dreary winter; she was an extra person for her aunt and uncle to feed and clothe; she knew she could teach children so she had a way to earn her keep.)*

Chapter 21 - Pages 239-249

Vocabulary:

dowries 239	illusions 242	governess 242
eluded 244	queried 246	ketch 246
unpremeditated 248		

Discussion Questions:

1. Summarize the novel using the story map on the next page. What purpose is there in a story map? How would using a story map help you as an author?

Story Map

A story map is just a simple drawing that helps you see how the important parts of a story fit together. It also helps you remember what happened in the story when talking or writing about it.

Fill in the story map.

1. Briefly describe the setting, or time and place, in which the story begins.

2. Describe the main problem.

3. Summarize at least three key events in the story.

4. Tell what the climax was. In other words, where was the point of greatest tension, where you knew the problem couldn't get any worse?

5. Describe the resolution, or what happened after the climax until the end of the

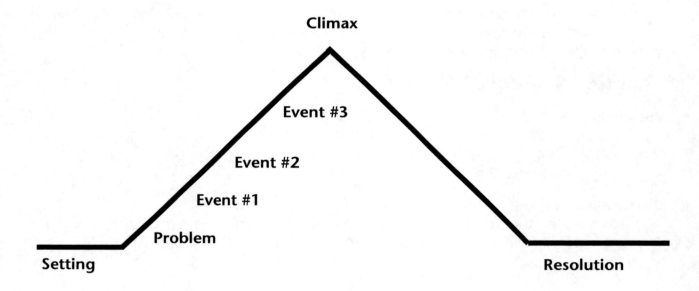

2. Is Kit a heroine? Why or why not? Brainstorm.

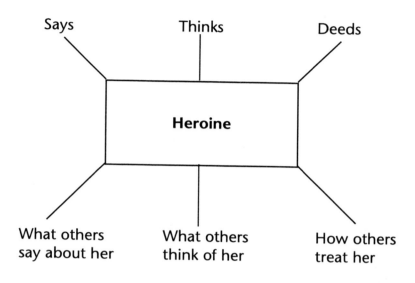

3. Explain the significance of the title of the novel. Does the Witch of Blackbird Pond refer to Hannah or Kit?

4. What was the author's message in this book? Why do you think the author wrote this story? What do you think is the most important thing to remember about this story?

Post Reading Activities

1. **Character Analysis:** Think about how Kit has changed during the course of the book. Fill in slots on the top line of the "map" on the next page with words or phrases which describe Kit during the first half of the story. Fill in the slots on the next line with words or phrases which describe her during the second half.

The
Story
Begins

The
Story
Ends

2. **Theme:** A central theme is an important message the author is trying to send about one of life's truths. What do you think the theme of this novel is? Put the theme in one sentence. Then write a composition that mentions specific incidents from the story that supports your theme.

3. **Plot:** Choose three events in the story, and write two or three paragraphs about how changing these events would have changed what happened in the story. For example, how might the story have turned out differently if:

   • Kit had married the older man in Barbados?
   • Kit had not rescued Prudence's doll?
   • Kit had not made friends of Hannah?

4. **Writing:** If you were to talk to the author, what questions would you ask her about the book? Make up a list of questions. Write the letter, address it, and send it.

5. **Writing:** What would you change about this story if you were going to write it? Why?

6. **Writing:** Do you think *The Witch of Blackbird Pond* is a good title for the book? Make up a new title for the story. Why did you give the story the title that you did?

7. **Comparison:** What other books, if any, have you read by this author? In what ways were they like this one?

8. **Art:** If you were the artist in charge of making three illustrations for the book, what three scenes would you illustrate? Use markers or paints to make the illustrations.

9. **Art:** Illustrate a new book jacket for *The Witch of Blackbird Pond*. Include a cover illustration, imaginary "rave review" blurbs on the back, and a short biography of the author (see your librarian for reference books containing summary biographies of

Assessment for *The Witch of Blackbird Pond*

Assessment is an on-going process, more than a quiz at the end of the book. Points may be added by the teacher to show the level of achievement. When an item is completed, the teacher and the student check it.

Name_____ Date _____

Student   **Teacher**

_____   _____   1.   Make a map of Kit's journey.

_____   _____   2.   Keep a simulated diary of Kit.

_____   _____   3.   Draw a portrait of one of the characters.

_____   _____   4.   Make an attribute web for one of the characters. (See pages 9-10 of this guide.)

_____   _____   5.   Make a Venn diagram to compare/contrast Judith and Mercy as prewriting for a short paper.

_____   _____   6.   Contribute to a model or mural of the village with the Meeting House, pillory, whipping post, and stocks.

_____   _____   7.   Complete one of the suggested research projects, Royalist-Roundheads, work of colonial men vs. women, cloth production, punishment for crime in the colonies, trade triangle, witchcraft in the colonies.

_____   _____   8.   Develop a sequence chart of the most important actions in the novel.

_____   _____   9.   Write a newspaper article that appears concerning Hannah Tupper or the hidden charter.

_____   _____   10.   Complete the heroine chart on page 41 of this guide. Is there a heroine in this novel? Why or why not? Write a short paper to develop your heroine chart.